Barges

by Lola M. Schaefer

Consultant:
Christopher Hall, President
Hall Associates of Washington, Inc.
Tugboat and Barge Brokerage

Bridgestone Books
an imprint of Capstone Press
Mankato, Minnesota

Bridgestone Books are published by Capstone Press
151 Good Counsel Drive, P.O. Box 669, Mankato, Minnesota 56002
http://www.capstone-press.com

Library of Congress Cataloging-in-Publication Data
Schaefer, Lola M., 1950–
    Barges/by Lola M. Schaefer.
    p. cm.—(The transportation library)
    Includes bibliographical references and index.
    Summary: Describes the history, early models, major parts, and jobs of barges.
    ISBN 0-7368-0502-8
    1. Barges—Juvenile literature. [1. Barges] I. Title. II. Series.
VM466.B3 S33 2000
386'.229—dc21   99-054150
                                                                                  CIP

Editorial Credits
Karen L. Daas, editor; Timothy Halldin, cover designer; Sara A. Sinnard, illustrator;
    Kimberly Danger, photo researcher

Photo Credits
A.B. Sheldon, 4
Archive Photos, 14, 16–17
Bruce Coleman, Inc./Jan Stromme, 6–7
David R. Frazier Photolibrary, 8–9, 18
Gary J. Benson, 20
Unicorn Stock Photos/Andre Jenny, cover
Waverly Traylor Photography, 10

1 2 3 4 5 6 05 04 03 02 01 00

Table of Contents

Barges

Barges are large, flat-bottomed boats. They carry heavy cargo from place to place. Barges cannot move themselves through water. Push boats push barges up and down rivers and canals. Tugboats pull barges along coasts.

cargo
goods that are carried
from one place to another

stern

deck

hull

bow

Parts of a Barge

A barge has a square-shaped hull. Workers place cargo in the hull or on the deck of the barge. The bow is the front of the barge. The stern is the back of the barge. Most barges have skegs on the stern. These fixed rudders usually are underwater. They do not turn.

hull
the main body of a boat

How a Barge Works

Workers tie a barge to a loading dock. They load cargo onto the barge's deck. Workers then tie the barge to other barges. Several barges together form a tow. A push boat pushes the tow along a river. Workers then unload the cargo at another loading dock.

9

push knees

Pushing or Pulling Barges

Push boats use two push knees to move barges along rivers and canals. These steel plates are on the bow of a push boat. Tugboats use ropes and cables to pull barges along coasts.

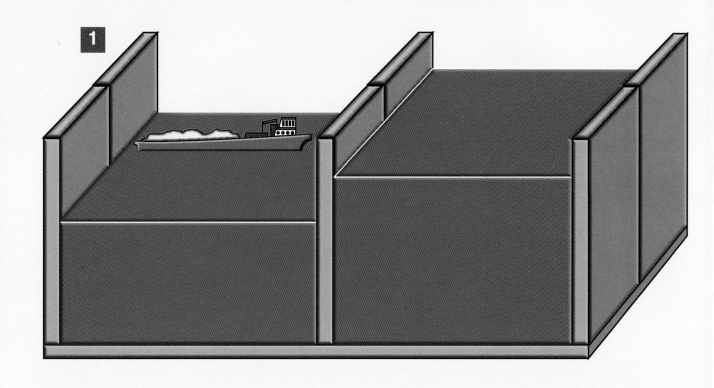

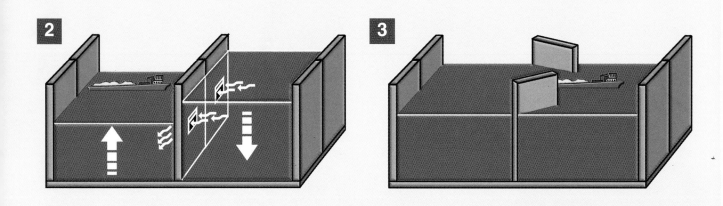

Barges and Locks

Locks help barges travel steep areas of rivers and canals. A barge enters a lock through a gate. Pumps and drains raise and lower the water in a lock. The water reaches the same level as the water in the next lock. The lock gate opens. The barge then moves to the next lock.

lock

an area of water with gates at both ends; locks help barges move from one water level to another.

The First Barges

The first barges were rafts. People tied reeds or small trees together to make rafts. Rafts carried cargo down rivers. They traveled with the current. Later, Egyptians made sailing ships. The sails helped push or pull these early barges along shores and through canals.

current
the movement of water in a river or ocean

Early Barges

People tied long ropes to each side of early barges. Horses and people on land used these ropes to pull barges. People also rowed barges to ships in harbors. These barges carried the cargo from the large ships into port.

port
a place where boats and ships can dock safely

Barges Today

Companies transport many goods on barges. Hopper barges carry coal, sugar, or grains. Deck barges transport pipes, small buildings, machinery, or cattle. One push boat can push a tow of 50 barges.

transport
to move people and things
from one place to another

Barge Facts

- The Panama Canal is a 50-mile (80-kilometer) long canal connecting the Atlantic and Pacific Oceans. A barge passes through six locks to move from one end of the canal to the other.

- One barge can carry the same amount of corn as 58 tractor trailers.

- Barges travel more than 1,800 miles (2,900 kilometers) on the Mississippi River from St. Paul, Minnesota, to New Orleans, Louisiana.

- Tows need more than one-half mile (.8 kilometers) to stop.

- Barges carried all of the equipment used to make the Trans Alaska Pipeline. This pipeline carries oil from the Arctic Ocean to Valdez, Alaska.

Hands On: Float and Carry

Barges carry heavy cargo across water. You can learn why it is easier to move cargo across water than across land.

What You Need

Foam meat tray
Table
Six forks
Sink half-filled with water

What You Do

1. Place the foam meat tray on the table.
2. Place six forks on the tray.
3. Use your finger to push the tray forward 6 inches (15 centimeters).
4. Place the meat tray in a sink half-filled with water.
5. Place six forks on the tray.
6. Use your finger to push the tray forward 6 inches (15 centimeters).

The tray moves more easily when it is in water. Water creates less friction than a solid object such as the table. Friction is a force that slows down objects when they rub against each other.

Words to Know

canal (kuh-NAL)—a channel dug across land to connect two bodies of water; barges carry cargo on canals.

cargo (KAR-goh)—goods that are carried from one place to another

engine (EN-juhn)—a machine that makes the power needed to move something

harbor (HAR-bur)—a place where ships unload their cargo

rudder (RUHD-ur)—a plate on the back of a boat used for steering; rudders on barges are called skegs; skegs do not turn.

transport (transs-PORT)—to move people or things from one place to another

Read More

Hill, Lee Sullivan. *Canals Are Water Roads.* Minneapolis: Carolrhoda Books, 1997.

Maynard, Christopher. *The Usborne Book of Cutaway Boats.* London: Usborne Publishing, 1996.

Schaefer, Lola M. *Tugboats.* The Transportation Library. Mankato, Minn.: Bridgestone Books, 2000.

Internet Sites

Hall-Tug
http://www.halltug.com
Island Tug and Barge Services
http://www.islandtug-barge.com/cargo.html
National Canal Museum
http://canals.org

Index